THE ILLUMINATED SECRET

THE
ILLUMINATED
SECRET

K. MASON

Dedicated to my son KMM Jr. aka "Chino." l love you dearly, boy. Every time I wanted to give up, all I could think about was you. Your essence has pushed me to my greatness. I did this for us. This is the foundation. Never depart from it. No matter what anyone says, I'll always be with you.

Michael "730" Corigliano – first and foremost you always said it, dawg, always telling people I'd make it. Man you inspired me so much. We talked about everything right, wrong, or indifferent. You held me down. Realest Italiano from Carnasie. "Can't Stop Won't Stop Billy," "Bad Ass motivation." Until we meet again, I know you are with me on every step. Rest in Paradise

Liz, oh Liz – let me tell you, I couldn't write a dedication without including you. You came in clutch. I don't know where you came from or why, but you did, regardless of our differences. A lot of this was made possible because of your spirit. Words can't express my appreciation. Life is short and unpredictable, so whatever happens, happens, but its forever till the "wheels fall off." Never forget: Positive thinking leads to positive results. Never stress over something that you can't change. But I know you got this. Thank you.

Li, we have had a lengthy history. Hopefully, no matter what, Mr. Amazing will never cease to Amaze. Thanks for everything.

TABLE OF CONTENTS

ONE

THE SECRET . . .

Despite my firm convictions, I have been
always a man who tries to face facts, and to
accept the reality of life as new experience
and new knowledge unfolds it. I have always
kept an open mind, which is necessary to the
flexibility that must go hand in hand with
every form of intelligent search for truth.

Malcolm X

Why is it that the truth never seems to be available
to the public? Why is it always hush-hush? Why is
it never given or readily available? Where is this
information kept and who knows these truths?

These questions often plague us, yet we are left in the dark. This book isn't just about exposing secrets; it's not about how to get rich quick. It's about understanding the sequence, understanding the truth, and being able to apply it. Yes, there are many texts, many books; you can read them all but never truly succeed without understanding and application.

By this point you're probably wondering, what is this big secret? What is the key that unlocks success? Well, before the secret is received, you have to understand certain things. You have to open your mind and receive it without bias. Malcolm X was very aware of this idea: he understood that in order to obtain knowledge and the truth, one has to remain open-minded and unbiased, and retain the ability to graph new thoughts. This is one of the most important rules: to remain open-minded and unbiased! This is the key to unlocking the secret. If you cannot do this or if you refuse to this, you will not succeed and your attempts will be futile. You will be wasting time you can never get back.

Flexibility. After receiving this information, you must be able to apply and use it, and this means being flexible. In fact, you need to be more than flexible; you must be formless:

> Empty your mind, be formless, shapeless
> – like water. Now you put water in a
> cup, it becomes the cup; You put water
> into a bottle it becomes the bottle; You
> put it in a teapot it becomes the teapot.
> Now water can flow or it can crash.
> Be water, my friend.
>
> *Bruce Lee*

Take a moment to allow this to penetrate your mind. This is a principle that most illuminated people hold valuable and true, and when reading this book you will begin to detect a trend and a pattern of the illuminated. They knew these secrets. They were exposed to these secrets and began to deliver them to the people, which led to their demise.

To apply the secret you must be able to do

anything, to be free mentally, since being free physically is not always possible. We all have responsibilities and other situations in life like marriage and children, being tied down to a job, or even incarceration, but once you allow your mind to be free and formless like water, all things are possible! And I can guarantee you, you are on the way to success and power.

It's easy to see that being open-minded and flexible can help you to become more intelligent and to obtain more knowledge and secrets. And you have to understand that succeeding in life is 90 percent mental and only 10 percent physical; I'll call this the 90/10 rule. Bruce Lee was the perfecter of this rule, as a very strong fighter and a very knowledgeable Kung Fu artist: before he defeated all of his opponents, he defeated them in his mind. Before you can defeat an opponent physically, you have to defeat them mentally, and the same goes for any other obstacles.

As children, most of us had vivid imaginations. We played with toys and personified them as if they were real; they were just objects, lifeless, but we built great scenarios where there was a story, a plot, a hero, and a villain, all in our minds. This was the rawest state of our mentalities, a creative state where we could make anything we believed come true. At that point in our lives we were young, we were small, and we weren't like our adult counterparts. If we go even further back in childhood to infancy, we can refer to the John Locke theory that states that when a child is born into this world, that child knows nothing, and everything that child sees becomes the building blocks to that child's mentality. In essence, we must return to the mind state of a child – fresh, open, creative, and ready to graph new thoughts and apply them. When I personally applied this to my life, I opened my mind to new things and applied them mentally, and then my life started to change.

As an example of how effective visualization can be, I once created a dream board (as an adult). I cut out many pictures from magazines of what I wanted to be and wanted to achieve. Many people mocked me as I had images of Rolexes, BMWs, men dressed in sharp suits, and a picture of a doctor. I felt that I wanted to be in the medical field and be very wealthy. At that time in my life I was incarcerated and many people made jokes and said I'd never reach those heights. I always smiled and remained objective, never taking offense . . . years later I owned several Rolexes, owned a home and a BMW, and had finished nursing school. It was a struggle to achieve these things due to my past, but I believed I could do it because I graphed those thoughts. I remained formless, convinced, committed to the process, and open to all possibilities, and I achieved it.

I credit this to the secret that was given to me by a very successful and illuminated individual who was able to enlighten me. I implore you to allow this information to saturate your mind. This is the way to the illuminated secret.

It can be hard for us to harness this ability of freethinking. In history there has been one group of people who have mastered this ability, and that is the Freemasons, a group of men who were dedicated to free thoughts and ideas. Classified as a secret society, they were shunned by people because they went against the grain of society's norms. You see, society can form a mental slavery that entraps people in a cycle like the rat race: go to school, get a job, pay bills, and die. Anything outside of this is seen as unusual or wrong, but why? There are many answers to this question, but remaining inside the lines isn't what life is all about.

STEPS

1. Open your mind.

    What is the first thing you do when you get up? Find a routine that invokes positivity, such as reading a motivational book, listen to motivating music, watch a motivational video or channel on YouTube, work out, run, jog, walk: this will set the tone for your day. When we first wake up, our minds are at their peak ability, refreshed and ready for the day. If we can condition our minds at this point, day in and day out, we can prepare to receive a seed that will plant, grow, and bear fruit.

TWO

RESILIENCY

I hated every minute of training, but I said,
"Don't quit. Suffer now and live the rest of
your life as a champion."

Muhammad Ali

The act of being resilient is being able to continue on and push through something hard without giving up. Michael Jordan's career is one the greatest stories of resiliency. Six-time NBA Champion, six-time NBA finals MVP, five-time most valuable player, fourteen-time NBA All Star (an All Star nearly the entire span of his basketball career), NBA rookie of the year, and the list goes on.

I could name at least 40 more accolades and awards, yet as successful as Michael Jordan has been, his career did not start that way. His first attempt on the road to becoming the greatest of all time resulted in him being cut from a basketball team . . . and as most humans do in the midst of failure, he cried, he wept, he bawled (literally). But soon after, he did something most people don't do. He tried again. But this time he prepared. He trained day and night, practiced jump shot after jump shot, dribble after dribble, calculated steps, he ran, he conditioned himself, he practiced so hard, and when he felt he just wanted to give up he pushed through and persevered. All he could see was the goal, the light at the end of the tunnel . . .

Resiliency was the key that unlocked the door to success, and as a result he will live out the remainder of his days on this earth as a champion, all because he didn't let a setback hold him back.

Fall down 7, stand up 8 is an expression often used to define resiliency. What does this term mean to you?

The Owl. The owl is one of the most resilient creatures in the world, among other characteristics and ideas associated with it. Interestingly, the secret society known as the Illuminati used this mystical creature as one of its symbols. The owl is one of the few creatures that adapts to almost any environment, and also one of the few birds that hunts its prey at night so that it cannot be detected by predators, which gives it a great advantage. What this animal lacks in intelligence and agility, it makes up in persistence, adapting and learning in any environment, ensuring its survival! This is a major key!

> Fail early, fail often, fail forward.
>
> *Will Smith*

Who would have thought the key to success was failure? Fortune favors failures because fortune favors the bold. To fail is to learn. The most successful people on this earth have had major failures, though their success visibly offsets their failure. The key to their success was resiliency and never giving up.

I remember when I was a child and I took the training wheels off my bike. I taught myself how to ride without them, but during my trials, I fell numerous times with that bike, scraping my legs, hurting my knees and bruising my arms. Day after day, I failed miserably but I never gave up, until finally one day I was able to ride down the block without falling. I was wobbly, but through all thoughts failure I finally learned how to ride without them. Breaking properly, though, was another obstacle, and with many foul-ups I finally learned how to overcome that as well. In essence, our lives are like learning to ride a bike, always falling, always injuring ourselves. But if we have enough determination and discipline, we can learn how to overcome our fears of falling and learn how to ride through life with ease. It may not be perfect. Even though we master those skills, we always have pot holes and mountains we have to ride through with our bikes. Thus, resiliency is the key to overcoming those challenges.

STEPS

1. Optimism is the number one rule to being resilient. You must think positive to receive positive results. You are what you think, what you eat, and who you associate yourself with.

2. Positive association. Connect yourself with other successful people, as these individuals may be able to give some great advice from experience and possibly point you in the right direction. If you aren't able to find these people to connect with, there is contact information in this book to reach out to network with others.

3. Take care of yourself. To recover from anything, one must have the resources, or have a foundation of good health from the beginning. For example, if you were to get seriously wounded, a doctor or dietitian would

advise you to add protein to your diet to aid in recovery. It helps the body regenerate cells faster and stronger. So having a good, healthy, consistent diet will help. And just as you feed your body, you must feed your mind: read healthy books, literature that reinforces positive thinking, put on positive music or videos, and listen to many success stories. They will aid you in becoming more resilient.

THREE

GROWTH

One can choose to go back toward safety
or forward toward growth. Growth must
be chosen again and again; fear must be
overcome again and again.

Abraham Maslow

When we think growth, we think heights, and with height comes phobia for some; actually, I believe that for most people, being in very high places and continuing to climb can be daunting. Imagine climbing the World Trade Center, which was one of the tallest buildings in the United States. It was 1,776 feet tall and 104 stories. Even the most brave individual would have fear of climbing that, but reaching the top means reaching success.

With growth, change occurs, and with change often comes discomfort. Growth is to comfort what oil is to water; they don't mix. For one to truly grow, one must stretch to new limits, new altitudes, and this can sometimes be strenuous, leaving the individual with a level of uncertainty which causes fear. We all fear the unknown.

In the Bible, Corinthians 2, verse 5:7 states: "Walk by faith and not by sight." What does this mean? We all have feelings inside us that can't be seen, like taste, hunger, smell, our emotions, etc., and we also have a yearning for success, to overcome adversity, and to achieve something. We can't physically see these things, only feel them. Natural growth relies upon the unseen forces that stretch us, and for us to continue to grow, we must gather that same innate ability to grow and go forward in life, without seeing but believing. We can compare this aspect of real life to a character's progress in a video game. You start at a basic level with basic attributes, but as you successfully complete each level, the level of difficulty increases, and with it the character's abilities and strengths, allowing you the chance to defeat or overcome obstacles in each new level. This is an example of how growth works in real life, and an ideology we need to apply in our lives.

Abraham Maslow, in *The Theory of Human Motivation*, describes the theory of human actualization, the need to become what we are meant to be, our ultimate and true selves. He discusses how our needs motivate us in this goal, in ascending order from the most basic (physiologic needs) to the most elevated (knowledge). Maslow's hierarchy of needs is often represented in the literature by a pyramid figure.

The pyramid, as a symbol, is one of the greatest mystical structures of all time and remains very mysterious. The pyramid was used by the ancient Egyptians to represent the steps to greatness with the very top as the gateway to heaven. This same figure is represented on the seal of the dollar bill, along with the All-Seeing Eye of Providence, which represents heavenly divinity and greatness. When you understand the meaning of the pyramid, you will understand growth, and why the Illuminati and other societies are associated with this symbol.

STEPS

Follow the steps of Maslow's hierarchy. Make sure that all of your needs at each level are satisfied so you can rise to the next. This will cultivate your growth and lead you to greatness:

1. Biological and physiological needs: Ensure that the needs of your physical body are satisfied in order to survive and thrive: food, air and water, a comfortable temperature, rest, sex, shelter, space, etc.

2. Safety: Protection, security, an ordered and predictable environment and life without unreasonable dangers.

3. Love and belonging needs: Emotional needs
    for love, acceptance, caring, friendship,
    and intimacy. This can include affiliation,
    belonging to groups, fraternities, teams, etc.

4. Self-esteem: this includes both confidence
    and a feeling self-worth and accomplishment,
    and the need for some type of recognition or
    respect from others.

5. Self-actualization: Creative accomplishments,
    realizing your true potential, self-fulfillment,
    personal growth and reaching heights, a
    desire to become what we are meant to be.
    (Maslow, 1987, p. 64).

Transcendence: After the fifth step, you reach the
Eye of Providence's greatness.

FOUR

DISCIPLINE

You can never conquer the mountain.
You can only conquer yourself.

Jim Whittaker

To me, this is the single greatest quote of all time. Jim Whittaker was the first known mountaineer to conquer and reach the summit of Mount Everest, the highest mountain in the world, located between China and Tibet. Take a moment to let this all saturate your mind.

Discipline is the single most important thing a person must learn to utilize and muster. This one factor can make or break a situation. Before Jim

Whittaker was able to accomplish this incredible feat, he had to understand that the true test was to be able to conquer himself, his own fear, resistance, weakness. This relates back to the skills and factors discussed in earlier chapters and all are all connected. To conquer yourself you must be able to open your mind and heart to making spiritual, mental, and physical sacrifices. Jim Whittaker's true challenge was with himself, not that mountain, challenging his own strength. The true battle is within ourselves.

If we look around, we notice successful people and we wonder how or why they achieved that success. There are so many things for us to obtain, a surplus it seems of mansions, Lamborghinis, private jets, yachts, exotic lands, desirable women or men, just to name a few of the luxuries we wish for, and they are all available to us. There will never be a shortage. We just have to discipline ourselves to obtain these things. The world and everything in it is yours.

When we think of the word discipline, we can

see that the root of the word is disciple. What does the word disciple mean to you? Jesus Christ had disciples, men who sacrificed their own wants to serve God for the greater good. The greatest disciple of Jesus was Peter, whose name in Aramaic language means "Rock." Even though Peter made incredible mistakes, he is still honored as the model apostle, considered the first pope and popes model themselves after Peter. Regardless of Peter's failures, he was so devoted and disciplined that he was willing to give up his own life for Christ. Later on, after Christ's death, he established the first church in Rome.

For years, groups and secret societies were persecuted for their free way of thinking, seeking the truth, and spreading it. The word Illuminati in Latin means the "enlightened ones." Jesus even speaks about the light: "You are the light of the world. A city on a hill cannot be hidden. Neither do people light a lamp and put it under a bowl. Instead they put it on its stand, and it gives light to everyone in the house. In the same way, let your light shine before men, that they may see your good deeds and praise your Father in heaven" (Matthew 5:14-16, NIV). Later, in the Gospel of John, "I am the way and the truth and the light. No one comes to the Father except through me" (John 14:6, NIV). By some, Christ and his disciples were considered to be evil for going against the grain, much as the secret societies are today.

How can one openly provide the light to the people without being persecuted and condemned? The answer is discipline. Through discipline, the message of Christ was still passed, and through his death, masses of people became illuminated . . . If one can harness the power of discipline, one can master almost anything.

STEPS

1. Start small, make minor changes one at a time and remain consistent, for example, if on a diet, choose not to eat at any more after 7 p.m., or 4 hours before bed. With time

your appetite before bed will decrease, and essentially, with the right diet, the size of your stomach will decrease.

2. To actually commit, one must be devoted to the process. Absolutely put in your mind that there is nothing else. You want whatever your goal is as much as you want to breathe, as much as you want to live. Give it your heart, your soul, your mind. Think it, dream it, eat it, watch it, read it, sing it. Completely and utterly immerse yourself in it like it's nothing else. Drown in it.

3. Focus. Give yourself tunnel vision: keep your eyes on the prize. Tune out outside distractions. Plan days off to sit in quiet and either think or work on the project or goal. ADHD and adult ADD are very prevalent in this day and age. Some people may need a prescription for medications that may aid in focus. Although most people don't agree with

the idea of medication, in this case it may be necessary to accomplish the goal.

4. Rest and relaxation. Have you ever noticed that monks are one of the most disciplined group of people? Their vocation requires that they meditate constantly, a form of relaxation and also a disciplined practice. When you are at your most calm, you are able to organize thoughts, plans, and be more efficient at working toward goals. If you wish to become more disciplined, meditation is one of the oldest forms of relaxation technique and has been effective for thousands of years.

5. Use incentives. Reward yourself when you have been successfully consistent with discipline.

FIVE

STRENGTH

That which does not kill us,

makes us stronger.

Friedrich Nietzsche

Pain, Power, Persistence . . .

Strength isn't limited to physical attributes and abilities. Strength is associated with mental capacity. I believe that life is 90% mental and only 10% physical, drawing from Stephen Covey's 90/10 rule, stating that 10% of life is made up of what happens to you, and 90% of life is decided by how you react. When you understand this and apply it to your life you can start to develop that inner strength.

Friedrich Nietzsche was a German-born philosopher who identified true strength through a concept he developed that he referred to as "Übermensch," meaning Superman or superior person. He proposed ideas that would help us develop a superior version of ourselves that involved great strength and ways to become stronger. When we think of Superman or Superwoman, we think of a creature with great power and strength, as depicted in comic books, far superior to regular humans. Friedrich believed that we each have our vision of a super version of ourselves. To identify this super version, we need to envision what we want most. What do you envy the most in others? Find the strength within to accomplish what you want most. These inner thoughts are the fuel that perpetuates the ability to evolve and become strong.

When a bone is broken, osteoclasts and osteoblasts, the cells that aid in bone repair, recreate bone tissue. During this process, the bone becomes stronger than it was before, more durable and tougher, as your cells work to prevent further breaks at that site again. This is a perfect example of something not killing a human but making them stronger.

Adam Weishaupt, like Friedrich Nietzsche, was a German philosopher, among other things. They shared some of the same ideas and interests and similar beliefs. Although they were in different eras, the message was eerily similar. They both believed that in order to secure real strength, one had to go against everything society believes in and conceptualize things for oneself: essentially, freethinking. Adam Weishaupt later founded the Bavarian Illuminati. Both of these philosophers' work later began to gain notoriety and is still relevant and observed till this day. It makes one wonder what type of power one could possess by understanding and conceptualizing these works. No wonder society wants to hide the truth from the people.

STEPS

Become mentally stronger

1. Find solitude. Even Superman had a "fortress of solitude." Solitude helps the mind relax, expand and create. Give yourself at least 15-30 minutes of quiet, allowing your mind to think and refer back to the previous chapters.

2. Challenge yourself once a week. Write out a task list and challenge yourself to complete at least one difficult task a week. If it isn't a task, it could be a goal or something that scares you. Do this once a week and in time you will develop greater mental tolerance. This will season you to be stronger.

3. Health is key. Even though your physical self is only 10 percent, build your health by eating well, sleeping, and working out to build a stronger mind. It has been documented

that certain foods like berries, nuts, and omega 3 fatty acids increase and improve brain function as well as memory. This may be how our ancestors millions of years ago advanced. Exercise also helps.

4. Be thankful! Talk gratitude, walk gratitude, think gratitude, express it to friends/family/strangers, post it on social media, write it down, record it. When acknowledging that you're grateful for success, even for the little things like life and food, mentally you are conditioning yourself, which reinforces your ability to be strong.

5. Give up bad habits one at time. It could be smoking cigarettes, eating meat, etc. This will increase your ability to be strong.

SIX

FOUNDATION

You can't build a great building on a
weak foundation. You must have a
solid foundation if you're going to have
a strong superstructure.

Gordon B. Hinckley

A foundation is a state of security, strength, endurance, and can be considered the backbone or the start of something; the beginning. Before a house can be built, a foundation must be laid and set, usually created with concrete or stone. If the foundation is not properly set, chances are the house may crumble or fall apart.

George Washington, the first president of the United States, also a Freemason, was essentially the mason that established the foundation of America. If we understand what "mason" means and incorporate that to the chapter, we begin to understand the mysterious secret in front of us.

How could one man, single-handed, build a foundation that has lasted over 220 hundred years and currently has a population way over a quarter billion people? That takes some hard work.

George Washington started a legacy and is always regarded as the father of America. How many of us can say they have a legacy that has such a strong foundation? Many people don't have the passion to build something so strong and firm.

STEPS

1. Passion. For one to ultimately create anything of value, whether physical or mental, one would have to have passion: the lust, the care, the love, the concern. All of these things are the ingredients to understanding whether

you have passion or drive for whatever you
are doing. If you have no passion whatsoever
in what you are building it would be wise
to abscond and abort the mission, because
careless mistakes will be made and all
may fail.

2. Conditioning. It was said that George
    Washington was in exceptional shape and
    excelled in most recreational sports, and was
    often commended for his incredible strength.
    This type of conditioning may have aided
    Washington in his many battles and led to
    him to be victorious in those grueling bouts
    where he was sometimes outnumbered. We
    must condition our minds this way.

3. Skill. Foundation-setting takes a certain
    amount of skill; this is where talent isn't
    necessarily important but skill is. Skill is
    obtained by experience, sometimes years of
    experience, but if we focus and concentrate
    hard enough, we may be able to supersede

the years of experience with continuous repetition and practice combined with the practices and the steps mentioned in earlier chapters.

4. Concentration. As mentioned before, the ability to focus on the task at hand and eliminate all distractions, including others' criticism when it is not constructive . . . if you know your craft and have experience and proven success, everyone's criticism isn't necessary in your life. Do your own thing and be creative.

5. Examination and perfection. Your foundation should be built and treated like a work of art. Put your heart into it, but also make sure you examine it and address any issues, fill any cracks, smooth out imperfections. You get one shot and if you build on a foundation with cracks, your house will surely crumble. Take pride in your work.

SEVEN

HIGHER POWER

I am intrigued by different religions and
respect them all, but to be honest, I feel
the most spiritual when I am doing yoga or
looking at an ocean. Being spiritual is feeling a
connection with a higher power and knowing
that life is about more than just achieving goals.
It is about feeling good in the moment.

Heather Graham

If we analyze this quote by Heather Graham, we realize that when she uses the phrase "More than ..."
she has identified a force, a feeling greater than herself. In this day and age, people identify with more
and more different religions and beliefs, and some
don't believe in anything at all. With the emergence

of technology and easier access to information, more people have sought for and derived their own opinion of religion and higher power. I believe that, due to the increased absence of belief in something greater than ourselves, productivity and success have decreased. I call this "Destruction based on improper interpretation" or "DBII." I see more and more of our generation destroying their state of mind with media, TV, Internet, etc. Excess use of media and technology limits the ability to interpret or reason, which I believe is decreasing the intelligence of our people.

Freemasonry has been labeled as an anti-God organization, but actually to become a member of the Masonic fraternal brotherhood, one must believe in a higher power and it can be whatever religion or belief one chooses.

I believe that this is an important factor for this organization. When one understands there is something greater than oneself, one provides work and effort that is selfless and more worthwhile, work that is for the greater good of humanity.

Understanding that you have a purpose, understanding that there is a task, a great mission, understanding your role in this life will guide you to your destination and bring you success. Success isn't always measured materially. Sometimes it is in how greatly you have inspired others or helped others make changes to improve and advance in life.

When you understand this, it doesn't matter what position you hold. You could be the janitor or the CEO, the dishwasher or the chef, every part of your job description will be worthwhile. Every toilet you clean, every dish you wash, every exotic dish you make, every check you sign, you will have the understanding that there is something greater than you and an ultimate purpose for your actions.

STEPS

1. Knowing yourself, being able to identify your true self, is a major key to establishing a mental foundation. To build yourself, you

have to know yourself, your weaknesses, your strengths, your character defects. You must understand what makes you "you." As mentioned in previous chapters, meditation and self-reflection are key to this aspect; these practices will give you a better map of yourself and aid in understanding the logistics of building a foundation. Understanding that there are things greater than yourself and reflecting on a higher power can give you perspective. This also helps in understanding yourself and your identity.

2. Preparation. Preparation is everything. If you fail to plan, you plan to fail. Every house and building is designed with blueprints or a plan. Planning things in advance allows you to set a strong, resilient structure. Sometimes preparation includes clearing your field; for example, a plane cannot land unless the coast is clear. Sometimes our blessings are stuck in

the air because of our environment; there is too much mess on the landing strip. There is always a great designer and there are greater things in the atmosphere that control our destination and aid us in where we land.

3. Self-compassion. Sometimes we have to give ourselves the empathy and compassion we deserve, not to feel sorry for ourselves for mistakes we've made but to credit ourselves for things we've accomplished. No need to seek approval from others! Be who you are, grow, learn, accept, and move on. Treat yourself to a vacation if you have worked hard. As a rule, there is no need to explain to anyone why and what you need. Sometimes we have to be compassionate with ourselves to know that we shouldn't allow people to continue to walk all over us and abuse us. There is something greater than ourselves that unconsciously directs us to listen to that inside positive voice.

4. Be childlike. Become a child once again. As a child we believed in the tooth fairy, Santa Claus, Superman, etc. We let our minds run wild with imagination, but they were the most productive days. We listened, we were ready and open to follow, we had that hope that in the future, everything would be all right. We need to return to this form to accept the fact of an omniscient spirit, all-seeing and all-knowing.

5. Mindfulness. Take time to meditate and reflect on a higher power or purpose. Remind yourself that there will always be some aspects of life that fall beyond your control, no matter how much you accomplish or how powerful you become. Accepting this will give you the peace of mind needed to concentrate and move forward.

EIGHT

DETERMINATION

Energy and persistence
conquer all things.
Benjamin Franklin

Determination is an internal character trait that involves being firm in one's efforts toward realizing a certain goal or accomplishing something. When one is determined to do or achieve something, focus and hard work are required. Nevertheless, being determined to attain a certain goal could become obsessive; in such a case, one would not be in a position to see the hitches. One ought to be aware, when determined to accomplish something, that there are numerous obstacles in the way; however, they ought not to hinder one from persisting.

Determination is a key character trait in an individual who is goal-oriented. For instance, when one has a project that is required to be completed in a certain period, determination would be a critical quality to help the person in moving forward and confronting any barricades that he/she could come across. A determined person has distinct characteristics and is able to harness their determination in ways central to their goal. Determination has particular relevance and significance that cannot be overlooked.

Characteristics of a Determined Person

The process of realizing one's objectives is not easy; thus, the aspect of determination is greatly required. Therefore, it is important to understand who is a determined person. This is someone who does not give up, irrespective of any situation. Determined persons comprehend that when they fall, they have to get up and carry on with their journey. Thus, giving up is an idea that cannot easily – or at all – appear in the mind of a determined person. Simply put, they are those persons who only believe in realizing the results of the set goals. The main feature of determined persons is that they go after what they need and comprehend that surviving is not adequate; thus, striving is the only way to maintain a perspective of determination.

A determined person is shorn of excuses and he or she is committed when this is done. This means undertaking their work irrespective of any barring forces. Determined people are always focused and think only about the future and the legacy they will leave behind; as a result, they strive to generate gains and build constantly on their achievements. Many believe that having several streams of income is crucial, and determined people like to be associated with individuals of like mind; for that reason, they normally avoid persons who are not goal-oriented. They are careful about their associations and any socializing they engage in outside of working hard so as to ensure that they are always leading by example.

Determination includes the ability to comprehend that change is inevitable; similarly, they learn easily and quickly and are able to adapt fast. Finally, determined persons comprehend that abundance is about more than money.

Major Ways of Harnessing and Upholding One's Determination

There are some key daily activities that can help you apply your determination to the job or jobs at hand. Ensuring that these activities are put in place requires prior planning, until they are established as a routine thing. Some people believe that not all humans are born with the character trait of determination, and that those that make it in life are simply the fortunate ones born with the character trait. However, this is not the case. Instead, those who succeed in life usually find ways to harness and apply what they have more efficiently and get the best out of it.

Planning for a day's work the night before
Before retiring to bed, it is useful to make key decisions regarding what to do on the following day. This includes what to wear and to eat. As a result, one avoids in advance some barricades in the way of accomplishing one's objectives for that day. This aligns with the process of adhering to one's daily budget. Thus, even the means of travel, if required, to get to the place of work should be considered. Primarily, planning on what to do in terms of work should be prioritized. The habit of planning one's day on the night before is central to avoiding time wastage and being sidetracked by insignificant things.

Executing the problematic things first
Difficult tasks require a lot of energy and input from the mind; thus, they ought to be attended to first thing in the morning when a person is fresh

and more energetic. After these are out of the way, we can relax and take care of the more routine work that doesn't require much in the way of mental strain, ability, and energy. Gaining self-control and accomplishing hard jobs sooner than later gives an individual a sense of gratification and emancipates energy that one would otherwise spend anticipating or being apprehensive about accomplishing them.

Disregard interruptions and time-wasters
Although various emergencies can arise when executing the planned activities, some things that come up will just be distractions and time wasters. Consequently, individuals ought to avoid them. Nonetheless, those things that need attention should be attended to in the shortest time possible. It is evident that by not responding to some issues, one sends a clear message that one is a sturdily-willed and focused individual. It is apparent that successful individuals have found the willpower to maintain concentration

on the most significant work first until its completion.

Restoring and maintaining one's energy
Taking a break from work when you feel the energy is fading is of great significance. It is said that "all work without play makes Jack a dull boy." Thus, taking a break re-energizes an individual to accomplish his tasks more efficiently and quickly. As well, renewed vigor and more finely tuned mental attention usually follow.

*Regularly remind yourself of your
ultimate objectives*
A reminder of what one is working to achieve is of great significance; this is because it serves as a motivator. It would be crucial to set aside a consistent time on a daily basis, perhaps for 5 to 10 minutes, towards visualizing the goals you've set. An emotional connection between the work to be done and the goals you wish to accomplish is of great importance towards their realization.

The Significance of the Character Trait of Determination in a Person's Life

Generating more focus and faith

By being determined, we become more focused. Thus, determination bears motivation that helps an individual to keep working towards attaining their goals. It is evident that the process of realizing one's goals requires confronting numerous barricades. Remaining focused and energetic to execute the tasks that are aligned with his/her goals necessitates a strong internal drive. All this is centered on the characteristic of being determined, as it helps to remain on track irrespective of obstacles and attention-seekers who could interfere with the process of attaining one's goals. Additionally, determined persons are said to have a lot of faith. Determined persons believe extremely strongly in themselves and their ability to succeed in life; this usually aligns with the process of realizing their set goals, especially in the short-term.

One becomes more positive

The determination perspective generates confidence in what one knows and believes one can achieve. When one is determined, positivity and optimistic qualities are evidenced as the underpinning of one's goals. Similarly, a psychological state is generated which allows one to realize one's aspirations. Positivity helps a determined individual to acknowledge his/her hard work and to keep moving forward.

One feels more in control

When we are determined, we place more emphasis on strategy and control all the interruptions that life puts in the path of our success. It would be foolish to deny that we all undergo insecurities as well as doubts; however, these should not be given space, except inasmuch as we can learn from them. Being determined helps us to carefully follow our plans within the specified timeframe.

Enhanced problem-solving skills

Determined people are always striving to achieve their set goals in a certain time limit. As a result, the various problems they face must be quickly solved in order to carry on with the main agenda of realizing their objectives. A state of cognizance of developed challenges and ongoing commitment to succeed means that future challenges offer the chance to execute the skills and knowledge acquired in the process of realizing one's objectives.

Enriched decision-making skills and clarity

Trust is vital in the decision-making process. It is developed from being determined in life. Decision-making is a critical ability that aids in implementing each day's tasks towards realizing one's goals. Steady reflection acts as a scope that can be applied to evaluate one's progress. By being determined, clarity is evidenced. This involves identifying one's objectives and planning how to execute them effectively. It is this developed clarity that enables an individual to concentrate and not be sidetracked from his/her goals.

It is evident that determination rules in the process of achieving one's goals. It is of such significance that without it, one cannot effectively direct the process of realizing his/her goals. When incorporated into the process and adhered to, determination makes it easier to attain the set goals. All successful people employ this character trait towards the goal of achieving prosperous lives. For that reason, people need to integrate this characteristic to their daily business; as a result, they will effectively realize their goals.

NINE

SUCCESS

It is better to fail in originality
than to succeed in imitation.
Herman Melville

Success is not final; failure is not fatal:
It is the courage to continue that counts.
Winston S. Churchill

Success . . . For a lot of people, the word "success" means a lot of things. Most people don't even know what it means for them or what it is for them. Right now you may be saying, "Oh yes, I do. I know exactly what it means to be successful. I know exactly what

I need to be successful." But do you really? Success for most people is being as rich and famous as celebrities; success for most people is simply having wealth or having what other people have. Many believe that their success can only be evident through these things. As Herman Melville said, "It is better to fail in originality than to succeed in imitation." Everyone has their own path to walk, therefore, everyone should have their own goals to accomplish. Follow your path. Achieve your goals, not someone else's. The problem with most of us is that we are constantly comparing ourselves and our achievements to those of other people. Often we question, why is that person more successful than I am? What most don't understand is that, in order to be successful, one must fail. Failure doesn't mean your journey has to end; failure simply means that you have to find another way to reach your goal. It's not the fact that we fail, it's how we react to that failure.

The only true failure is not to use that failing experience as an opportunity to learn and to become better at what you do. Arianna Huffington is one of the most recognized names in the online publishing sector. But before she achieved this status, she too failed. Her story started with the dream to go to Cambridge. Even though that happened for her, her dream of becoming a writer did not come without its challenges. Rejection came after rejection, but she didn't give up. She got rejected by 36 publishers; 36 times she failed, but yet she never gave up. She never decided that this would not work out and she should just do something else, something safe. She just never gave up on her dream.

So many people are scared of failing, but as William Churchill said, "Success isn't final, failure isn't fatal, but rather it is the courage to continue that counts." Bill Gates is another success story who had also failed. His first company, where he partnered with Paul Allen, was a complete failure. He had to sit and watch that company fail. But that didn't stop him. He began exploring and experimenting with different ventures, and a few years later, he created the Microsoft product. Now he is considered to be one of the richest individuals in the world. If Bill Gates or Anna Huffington had resorted to comparing themselves to other entrepreneurs, they might never have gotten to where they are today.

Taraji P. Henson, a popular actress with starring roles such as Cookie in the HBO series *Empire*, began her journey at 26 years old, when she moved to California with her toddler and $700 in her pocket. Many people told her she couldn't do it. Many people told her she was too old, many people told her she would fail and she would have to move back home. But Taraji P. Henson had her dream and she wanted to achieve it. She didn't listen to the naysayers; she didn't listen to the constant negativity around her. She had placed a goal in front of her and she was determined to be achieve it: "I wasn't born with a silver spoon in my mouth. I had a passion, I had a dream, and I [dove] in and I went for my dream."

At 47 years old, she said she is just now hitting

the surface of the successes that she intends to achieve. In an interview with Goalcast, she said her passion kept her moving. She had a dream and she went for it.

The question that you might be asking now is, "How do I become successful?"

STEPS

1. A lot of people take success to mean a lot of money. Money, most of the time, is just the icing on the cake. True success comes after achieving a goal you have set a for yourself, based not only on what others have accomplished, but based on your passions and what you love.

2. Do not compare yourself and the speed of your success to others. As the famous saying goes, "the race is not for the swift, but it is for those who can endure." Comparing yourself to others will always make you feel like a

failure, even when you're not failing at all. As Taraji P. Henson said, "If you listen to other people . . . you won't live." Self-comparison is the key to failure.

3. Don't be afraid to risk. All the success stories of accomplished individuals have in common that those people took risks. All of them believed in their dreams and not what others told them. Steve Harvey once said: "If you do what you've always done, your life will never get better." To be successful, risks are a must, because most of the time success seems like the impossible.

4. Don't let failure paralyze you. You will experience failures while on the journey of achieving your goals. Many people hate to hear the word "failure," but the truth is, failure is the driving force towards success. Don't go living in a bubble believing that if you fail, that means it wasn't meant to be.

If you fail, that means that there is simply another way or method to achieve that particular goal. Try again. Try a different approach. Analyze what you did wrong and learn from it. No one ever became successful by giving up on their goals. They became successful by trying and trying and trying again, even when they were told that they were wasting their time. They blocked out all the negativity and they went after their goals, and eventually, they were successful.

5. To help you find your motivation, surround yourself with like-minded people, read motivational stories, listen to inspirational songs. Do whatever you have to do to keep your mind focused on your particular goal.

TEN

MONEY

Do what you love and the money will follow.

Comfort and accessibility to various amenities in life are what most people want. The way to access these comforts and amenities is through the use of money. Safety and security is also important to most of us, and money is the medium through which these things can be provided or obtained. Money also ensures that one receives the best healthcare If needed. Money provides us with the basic necessities in life and the truth of it is, most, if not all of us, want more of it. There is no shame in that. The only shame is the love of money to the extent that one would do anything, hurt anyone just so that they can get more of it.

We can also look at it to say that we only go to school so that we can get a good job that pays well, and with this well-paying job, our egos will be taken care of and we will feel secure and safe. Again, there is no shame in this. Everyone wants to live comfortably, as this relates to achieving material things. The stress of life is felt most by those who have little or no money to support themselves, and so money is always being chased after by us human beings. But the fact of the matter is, many people, for various reasons, don't have access to the amount of money that they would like to have. For some, their job doesn't pay enough and they have to live from paycheck to paycheck, even though in most cases they don't love their jobs as much as they should.

Many wish they could increase their earnings so that they can feel more comfortable and secure, but they have no idea how.

One option is starting a new business. You

might read this and begin thinking, "Oh no, not another business development idea." But the truth is, entrepreneurship is one of the best ways to increase your income and your growth. Yes, it's easier said than done. It's even a very risky venture, and the truth is, you might not succeed on the first try. However, it means that you'll be able to control the amount of money that you make.

Another method to increase your income is by joining an online platform. An option is to seek telecommunications jobs where you can work from the comfort of your own home. It doesn't have to be a full-time position, but it can be part-time where you can be sure of some extra income. Another online method for extra income earning is to teach English online. These platforms only require a few simple steps and instructions where you can earn up to $25 USD per hour. This is a lot of extra money that could come in useful. Another online option is to become a freelancer in various trades. These include writing, graphic design, data entry, video production, and consultancy.

There are many options, all dependent on what your skills and assets include. Virtual assisting is also another growing industry where you are paid to be an assistant, but over the Internet. Not only is it doable, but it also pays quite well.

A second job is also a way of earning extra income. It sounds harder than you'd like it to be, but after you've placed yourself in a better position, you can go into other ventures. Investment is also a great way to earn extra income. You can do this by putting a small amount aside, as investment does not necessarily require large amounts. You can even invest two dollars, whether in a friend's business, other businesses or through stocks and trading. Before either of those ventures are attempted, however, you need to make sure that that option is the right choice for you.

As Virgil once said: "Fortune sides with those who dare." This means that in order to achieve or make more money, you will have to take risks. As scary as this might sound, it is necessary. Money is easy to lose, but you can determine how much you lose, and how fast you are able to re-earn that lost amount of money. While you are trying to find ways of earning extra income, it is also important to note how necessary saving is. Even if you can only afford to save ten dollars per week, ensure that you are saving as much as you are able. This may require you to budget and refrain from buying things that you may not need. For example, if you are accustomed to ordering take-out food five times a week, try to cut that done to at most two times a week.

Whatever amount you were able to keep from that reduction, add to your savings every week, and you'll be surprised at how quickly your money can grow. People often believe that they are unable to save because they don't make enough money, but when you cut unnecessary spending, you can save a lot of money. Even after you've found a great way to increase your earnings, also ensure that you are putting some aside for unfortunate events that may happen at any time.

In addition to this, it's never too early to start

saving for your retirement. Retirement funds can determine how comfortable you are when you've reached a certain age and are unable to work. While you're saving for your retirement, your retirement fund is also earning money for you as over the years that money will attract a certain amount of interest.

You can also save your loose change. Don't be surprised when at the end of the year, you've garnered over five hundred dollars in emergency funds just from that loose change you decide to save.

Practice saving. It will eventually become a habit that will stick with you if you allow it to. Money is important, and not having a lot of it can be stressful, but finding new ways to earn extra and even save can be the lifesaver you never expected.

ELEVEN

INCARCERATION

For to be free is not merely to cast off one's chains, but to live in a way that respects and enhances the freedom of others.

Nelson Mandela

I was once incarcerated. For many people, incarceration has always been a sore point that no one wants to discuss. It's almost taboo to talk about incarceration or people who have been incarcerated, as it has been seemingly forgotten that the incarcerated are people too. The sad part is, even the incarcerated sometimes forget that they are people too, even though incarceration is supposed to be aimed at ensuring that the incarcerated are rehabilitated and can become beneficial to society. Regardless of the crime or crimes committed, everyone deserves a second chance.

As much as it may seem like it, incarceration doesn't mean the end of your life. You are still able to live and make something more of yourself, even if you were given a death sentence. You have only decided to stop living once you give up on life.

Take the story of Michael G. Santos, who was imprisoned at 23 years old for selling cocaine. For this crime, he received a 45-year sentence in 1987. He didn't quarrel with the system, neither did he blame others for where he ended up. Instead, he accepted the responsibility for the choices that he had made. His mindset and his determination to fully develop himself in becoming the good citizen he was expected to be resulted in his being eligible for release in 2013.

While serving his prison sentence, he studied for a bachelor's degree at Mercer University. In 1992, he graduated with honors, and in 1995, he received his master's degree from Hofsta University. However, these successes did not come without their challenges. While he was on the track to improving himself, he experienced heavy resistance from the system. He didn't let this deter or stop him. Instead, he turned his attention to establishing programs and writing resources that could benefit the other inmates and their families by helping them to adapt to life in prison. All this he did while attempting to study for his doctorate. His support came from his wife, who would help him to type his manuscripts; this helped him to develop his volumes of books, including the well-known *Inside: Life Behind Bars in America*. In addition to this, he also writes daily blogs for the *Huffington Post* where his work and writings are now widely used as a source for university and college courses related to penology and criminal justice.

Nelson Mandela is another awe-inspiring story of a prisoner who overcame his circumstances. In 1962, he was arrested for planning to overthrow the state. He was sentenced to life imprisonment.

He ended up serving 27 years in prison, as he was released only in 1990. In 1994, Nelson Mandela and F. W. de Klerk began negotiations to terminate apartheid. This resulted in the development of the multiracial general election where Mandela was elected president. He went from prisoner to president.

Think about his mindset while he was in prison for 27 long years. For most of us, this length of time behind bars is unimaginable, but after 27 years, it seemed that Nelson Mandela's mindset was even stronger than before. He negotiated, successfully, with the government to put an end to institutionalized racial segregation and discrimination, after which he became president. He became South Africa's first black head of state and also the first to be elected in a fully representative democratic election.

Neither Nelson Mandela nor Michael Santos gave up on their lives, even as they faced unimaginable years and lifetimes in prison. They both used their time behind bars to study and teach others, and with this mindset were able to overcome their circumstances and obtain early release. They both kept the faith, kept their minds focused on being better people, not only for themselves, but also so that others, even strangers, could benefit.

For those who are in prison at this moment, hold on, and for those who have been released, believe that you can be better and you will be. Prove to people that you can be more than they expect you to be, because the truth is, once someone living on the outside discovers that a particular individual has been released from prison, there is an immediate sense of fear and judgment regardless of the crime or crimes that were committed. Most civilians, in fact, don't care what the crime was, all they know is that this person was incarcerated, so they think he/she must be a bad person.

For the soon-to-be-incarcerated, the incarcerated, and the released, don't buy into these notions. You can prove to them that you are more than your past. You will face difficulties and challenges. It will be hard to find jobs, a place to live where you won't be constantly judged as you go about changing your life for the better, and of course, it will be hard to find true, good, real friends.

STEPS

1. Set goals and keep focused on those goals. Don't give up. Giving up would mean that you've given up on yourself, that you believe that there is no hope for you. But there is always hope.

2. Keep believing that you are more than other people's perception of you, that you are better than what you thought you were. Opinions, your own or other people's, do not define you or what you may become in the future.

3. As Nelson Mandela said, "For to be free is not merely to cast off one's chains, but to live in a

way that respects and enhances the freedom of others." Being respectful even when you aren't being respected is hard, but this will not only show your good character but will also prove to society that you are more than worthy of respect.

4. To the public: Don't "write off" anyone who has been incarcerated. It's not up to us to determine who remains free and who does not. It is up to us, however, to be an example to others. Be positive, not destructive. Consider the feelings of that person you are judging. Consider what it must have felt like while they were incarcerated and now that they are released, how much more difficult it will be for them to survive in the open world. You can even try to encourage them, as difficult as this might be. You may never know how much you will be able to change their lives just by a few meaningful words.

5. As I mentioned earlier, I personally was
    incarcerated at one point in time and I turned
    it all around. I used that negative energy and
    converted it to positivity. I earned degrees
    and professional licenses, became a nurse,
    and later on opened a few companies.

TWELVE

COMEBACK

Regaining Everything after Losing Everything

You gain strength, courage, and confidence by every experience in which you really stop to look fear in the face. You are able to say to yourself, "I've lived through this horror. I can take the next thing that comes along."

Loss: the word sounds sad and ugly, but the truth is, it can happen to anybody. Although it isn't anything that anyone would want to experience, we can become better persons as a result of our losses. Our achievements are important to us, as are our family and friends. Imagine losing a career, friends, and maybe even family members, but then imagine regaining all those things in a different way and under better circumstances. It may seem like it at first, but losing everything is not the end of the world. A part of your world may have seemingly ended, but you can begin again, and with faith and persistence, your life can feel whole again.

Donald Miller, who is an American author, business owner, and public speaker, once posted a blog that he wrote, which he titled, "Why losing everything could be the best thing for you." Seeing that title you may wonder how losing everything could turn out to be the best thing for you. Ridiculous, right? No, it's not. Donald Miller told his story and how there were periods in his life where he experienced so much loss that all he could feel was pain. Although he did not mention what those losses were, it is without a doubt true that he suffered. He mentioned that he had become a better person just because he experienced all that pain and sorrow. He also went on to say that his work ethic is much stronger than it was before. His faith has also grown and he is able to make more rational and better decisions. And this all happened just because he once lost everything.

His message doesn't stop there. He says that feeling as if you've lost everything can put you in a very bad and dark place, but believing that you're in that position for a reason can allow you to learn. He mentioned how much he had learned from those losses, especially the third one, that related to his business life. He looked deep within himself asking the question of how this loss could be useful to him. As it related to his business loss, it taught him how to more efficiently and effectively operate his business. He became more disciplined towards work, he was more humble and he had learned that possessions and status were not the most important things in his life.

You can imagine that he probably also lost friends, maybe even family, but he grew from those experiences and became a better person. He still does motivational public speaking and shares his beliefs and his inspiration both in speech and writing through his well-received books. His businesses are thriving and his personal life also seems to have also improved drastically. Angelina Jolie once said, "I do believe in the old saying that what doesn't kill you makes you stronger. Our experiences, good and bad, make us who we are. By overcoming difficulties, we gain strength and maturity." Donald Miller is living proof of that, and you can be too.

Martha Stewart also has an inspirational story where she had seemingly lost everything, but then regained it all. Martha was and still is known as the first American self-made female billionaire. After getting married and having her daughter, she went to work as a stockbroker for a firm known as Monnes, Williams and Sidel. Later, Martha decided to turn her attention on gourmet cooking after training herself through the written works of Julia Child. She then established her catering business, Martha Stewart Inc., which grew to be worth a million-dollars within 10 years.

She later expanded into the writing industry.

She experienced her first loss in 1990 with her divorce. She and her husband had been married for 29 years. A year later, the name of her company changed from Martha Stewart Inc. to Martha Stewart Living Omnimedia Inc. The release of her magazine, *Martha Stewart Living*, grew to include two magazines, a checkout-size recipe publication, a popular cable television show, a newspaper column, a series of how-to books, a radio show, and an internet site, all of which garnered her 763 million in annual sales.

In 1999 she went back to Wall Street so that she could guide her company through its first public offering in the New York Exchange. Her 72 million shares jumped to approximately $130 million dollars. At that point, her company was worth 1.2 billion dollars.

After so many successes, in 2002, an investigation surrounding Stewart led to allegations that she had sold hundreds of shares of ImClone Systems just before the Food and Drug Administration refused to approve the company's new cancer drug.

Based on these allegations, she was forced to resign from the board of directors of the New York Stock Exchange only four months after she had become a member. In 2004, although one charge was dropped, she was found guilty of conspiracy, obstruction of justice, and two counts of making false statements. She was then given five months in a low-security prison along with a 30,000-dollar fine. She had seemingly lost everything.

One can well imagine that she lost friends at this time, not to mention the divorce from her 29-year marriage not so many years before. One can imagine the turmoil that she went through, the emotions that she was experiencing and the feeling of loss and utter failure. But her mindset remained strong, and after her release in 2005, she was slated to be the host of two new shows, namely a spinoff of *The Apprentice* along with a how-to show. Regardless of her imprisonment, her company still continued to grow along with various publications she had created. She experienced many other failures after that, but she didn't give up. Instead she found other ways to succeed.

Loss is a terrible experience for anyone to go through, but you can rise again and become a better person in all areas of your life. Tragedies may happen at any time, but all that counts is how you react towards such loss or tragedy.

THIRTEEN

WINS AND LOSSES

You have to be okay with wins and losses.
You can't just be looking for the wins and
when the losses happen, you can't buy more
and more because you're sure it's going to
bounce. We call that revenge trading.

Josh Brolin

The loss just made me hungry; it made me
want to go out and win another title.

Thomas Hearns

It's always great when you're winning, but sometimes we get so accustomed to winning that we are

not mentally or otherwise prepared for losses. We have to accept that winning and losing are parallel to each other and either one can be the ending sentiment. However, what we also need to remember is that neither is permanent. What is more important is how we react in any event. A loss isn't a permanent thing. If you lose, the ideal thing is to get up and try again. Not to get up will be where you'll experience the biggest and most terminal loss.

More than that, a loss can be as important as winning, arguably more important. Losing can teach you so many things, a new game play, for example, or correcting a mistake that could lead to winning. The truth is that no one wants to lose at any given time, but sometimes losing is necessary. If you are always winning, you'll become too comfortable, believing that you will always win, and when you lose and you're devastated, you will not know how to recover. However, in losing, you're able to get back up again, revisit the drawing board, and try again. Thomas Hearns is no stranger to losing, but according to him, his losses just simply made him even more hungry to win.

Many successful persons have experienced losses throughout their journey, but how they reacted to these losses was the determinant of how their lives eventually turned out.

Jennifer Hudson, a famous actress and singer, lost her mother, her brother, and her nephew within three days after her estranged brother-in-law shot and killed them in a fit of rage. You can imagine what she was going through mentally. But did these tragic losses keep her down? No. She mourned, then she got up and started a foundation in honor of her nephew. In spite of all of this, she even learned to forgive her brother-in-law for what he had done.

Before Nicole Kidman had a family, she suffered from infertility for a long time. She had miscarriages, an ectopic pregnancy, and fertility treatments. She could have told herself that she would never be able to become a mother, but she refused to accept that statement. She simply won in another way. She adopted two children, after which she gave birth to two daughters.

Sometimes losing can cause you to believe that there is no hope, but if you believe that you can recover, you will, and then you'll become a better person as a result of it. If you lost one way, go back to the drawing board, figure out what went wrong, fix it, and then WIN.

There are so many other stories that one could draw from about how successful persons took their losses and turned them into wins. Here's another way of looking at it: instead of looking at them as losses, look at them as opportunities. Consider them opportunities to become better, personally and professionally.

STEPS

1. Respect. Accept the loss for what it is, even respect it, and learn from it. Figure out how you can use that loss to your advantage. Think about how that loss can become useful

to you in any way possible. Keep pushing, keep believing and you'll be able to win even after you believed you had lost everything. Respect these losses as opportunities and you'll be able to turn that opportunity into a win.

2. A loss can forever alter your perspective whether it be for the good or the bad. How it changes your perspective is entirely up to you. Changing your perspective for the good is always looking at the big picture, always staying focused on what's ahead and not necessarily what has happened or what is happening. Never be so focused on what is happening in the now that you ultimately forget what could happen in the future.

3. Know when giving up is the right thing to do. You might be now asking, "How could such a thing be suggested? Giving up should never be an option!" and in a sense you might be

right, but remember the idea of perspective change. Sometimes constantly going at something in a particular way is a lost cause, but many times we fail to see that because we don't want to be known as the one who gave up. But sometimes, giving up, or better yet, changing directions is the best decision to make if you want to keep your sanity intact. It could also mean that changing direction was the best decision to make as it placed you right on the path of success. Try to identify when it is time to give up on that one thing. There's no shame in that. If you've tried a plan numerous times and it failed on all occasions, pause, think, and make a change. Try to find a way through or even over a particular barrier and you'll eventually win.

4. Don't be so comfortable winning that you've forgotten that losses can occur and how to move on from one. It's important to be prepared mentally and otherwise in case of a

loss. Don't be fooled into believing that there can only be wins, as this is a delusional way of thinking. Instead, hope to win, but also be prepared if you should lose.

5. Learn. Every loss comes with experiences and new knowledge. To win again, you need to think about the loss. How did it happen? Can anything be changed to correct this problem? How can you use this loss to gain? Sometimes it's hard to look back on our failures or our most painful moments, but sometimes it's also necessary if you want to succeed in something.

Winning is great, but losing sometimes can turn out to be even greater.

FOURTEEN

MILLION-DOLLAR MINDSET

You cannot have a positive life
and a negative mind.

Joyce Myer

Scientists, spiritualists, and regular people alike will tell you that they consider the mind the most powerful free tool a human has. In reality, the world is filled with energies and vibrations; this, even the physicians have agreed with. Believe it or not, thoughts are tangible things, as they can frame either the tragedies or triumphs of your life. People who have found success will tell you that what kept them going and determined was their mindset, which eventually led them to their pot of gold. Their million-dollar minds kept them going and believing that they would eventually find their success. They would certainly agree that the mind is the key to success, but it can also be the cause of one's downfall. In the quest for success, we rarely focus on our mindstate or the strengthening of our mind, often instead our focus is on chasing "the dream," forgetting that the mind is the tool that is most likely to help us acquire that dream.

Oprah Winfrey is now one of the richest women in the world, but she wasn't born that way. She was born to a single mother and grew up on her grandmother's farm. When her mother finally got work, she moved to Milwaukee, where her mother worked as a housemaid. When she was left at home each day, she was repeatedly abused by two boys. This abuse lasted until she was thirteen years old and at fourteen years old she was on her own in the great big world. If that weren't enough, it turned out that she was pregnant, but the baby died in childbirth.

Imagine the emotional struggles she must have been going through; imagine the strength of her mind to have survived that trauma.

At seventeen years old, Oprah Winfrey won a beauty pageant, after which she was given the opportunity to be on air. This turned out to be the turning point of her life. She spent a lot of time as a news anchor until she was invited to be the host of a morning show.

In less than one year, the show had become one of the most popular shows on television. Renamed *The Oprah Winfrey Show*, it became an hour long special each day. After 1986, Oprah's show began to win many awards and went national. Her million-dollar mindset got her to where she is now, the owner of her own television network, among other great achievements.

Her mind had to be strong to pull her through the traumas that she had been through. She must have unknowingly been training her mind to always be thinking positive even while she was surrounded by constant negativity. She had to be careful of what she was thinking, because thinking negatively could have adversely affected her outcome. Recurring negative thoughts could have sent her into a downward spiral and her life might have turned out much differently. She didn't accept that her fate was to remain an assault victim or a detainee.

She didn't allow her mind to wander. She kept her focus, she kept the power in her mind, and refused to let her circumstances decide her future. Negative thoughts will cross our minds, but that doesn't mean that we have to hold on to them.

You have the power to decide what thoughts remain in your mind and what thoughts don't. If you give negative thoughts the chance to take root, they will, and then they will cause havoc and erode your strength of mind. Your thoughts affect you and your actions. Whatever you decide to focus on is what will come to you. Focus on negativity, and you will constantly attract negativity. However, if you focus on positivity, on success, you will attract positivity and success. As Joyce

Myer said, "You cannot have a positive life and a negative mind."

Many people refuse to believe the power of the mind, but don't be fooled, the mind controls the energy that surrounds us, whether negative or positive. We decide which energy we want to be surrounded by based on the thoughts that we constantly harbor. If you feel stuck, you can make changes in your life by changing the way you use your mind.

STEPS

1. Give your mind the credit that it deserves. Your mind is more powerful than you think, more powerful than you may be able to comprehend. The world operates on energies and vibrations, and therefore your mind can determine the energies that surround you.

2. Focus on positives so that you can attract positives. Focus on success and you'll attract

success. Your mind is powerful. Don't forget that.

3. Don't keep your energy focused on trivialities. Instead, train yourself to focus your mind on what you want to achieve and how you'll be able to do that. We often forget that our minds can break us as well as build us.

4. If you want to change your situation, you have to first change your mindset. Let it be positive thoughts that dominate your mind, not the other way around. In order to change what is happening on the outside, you first have to change what is happening on the inside. Train your mind to think about good health, success, prosperity, and happiness. If your mind is always focused on these things, then there is no doubt that your negative environment will turn positive.

5. The people that surround you can also affect the way that you think. If you keep positive thinking people around you, your mindset will always be positive. On the other hand, keeping negative people around you will no doubt turn your mindset negative. Always surround yourself with people who will be able to build you up.

By keeping your mind trained on positive thoughts no matter what happens, you can rise above any circumstance. This, combined with determination and a disciplined life, will help you achieve your goals. This is the million-dollar mindset and the key to great success.

CLOSING WORDS

Hopefully you have read this book in its entirety, and if you did then you have been able to receive a lot of tips, steps, and secrets, but this book mainly points to a number one secret that all successful people have been using for many, many years. If you haven't already figured it out, the secret is complete open-mindedness and observation, not necessarily using your eyes, but using all of your senses: touch, smell, taste, sound, and vision, and then transmitting all of that information to the most important part of you – the brain. People often refer to this location as the third eye because it involves observation and analysis of all that you take in from your senses.

To be able to truly apply these things to your life successfully, you have to receive life with an open mind, unmasked. You must remove the blind fold from third eye, completely remove everything you have ever learned and been taught, and analyze all observations without bias, completely objectively. Then you will finally been able to understand the secret that only the smallest percentage of the world uses and applies. Then you, my friend, will be on top of this illusion of the world we live in. Become illuminated.

For more information on this author

and available products, check out:

www.Kmasonmotivates.com

Follow on:

@kmasonmotivates

@kmasonmotivates

@kmasonmotivates

@kmasonmotivates